Mammals

by Kelly Gaffney

raintree
a Capstone company — publishers for children

Engage Literacy is published in the UK by Raintree.
Raintree is an imprint of Capstone Global Library Limited, a company incorporated in England and Wales
having its registered office at 264 Banbury Road, Oxford, OX2 7DY – Registered company number: 6695582

www.raintree.co.uk

Editorial credits
Gina Kammer, editor; Richard Parker and Peggie Carley, designers;
Pam Mitsakos, media researcher; Tori Abraham, production specialist

Image credits
Getty Images: Merlin D Tutle, 22 middle left; Minden Pictures: Hiroya Minakuchi, 15, Ignacio Yufer/FLPA, 13, Ingo
Arndt, 1, Mary McDonald/NPL, 21, Mike Parry, 22-23 bottom; Science Source: ANT Photo Library, 18 bottom right,
Friedrich Saurer, 8; Shutterstock: Andreas Weiss, 17 top right, BMJ, 23 middle left, ChameleonsEye, 23 middle right,
Chris Moody, 16-17, Christopher Wood, 10-11, Claudia Paulussen, 4 bottom right, Colin J D Stewart, 4 middle right,
Ethan Daniels, cover middle left, FloridaStock, cover middle right, Graeme Shannon, 7, Igor Stramyk, 5, Lovely Bird,
18-19, Luke Shelley, cover bottom middle, Manuel Findeis, 4 bottom left, mexrix, design element, Michael C. Gray, 20,
nulinukas, 6, Panu Ruangjan, 4 middle left, Tony Rix, back cover, Tosaphon C, 4 middle, tratong, 14, tsuneomp, 9,
Vladimir Melnik, 12, Wolfgang Zwanzger, 10 bottom left

10 9 8 7 6 5 4 3 2 1
Printed and bound in China.

Mammals

ISBN: 978 1 4747 3166 9

Contents

What is a mammal?

All living things can be put into groups. When scientists are deciding which group an animal belongs to, they put animals that are alike together. Scientists have put all the animals in the world into five main groups. The groups are birds, fish, reptiles, *amphibians* and mammals. We belong to the group known as mammals.

birds

fish

reptiles

amphibians

mammals

Many farm animals, such as pigs, are mammals.

There are over 4,000 different types of mammals in the world. Many farm animals, such as cows, pigs and goats, are mammals. Some of our favourite pets, such as dogs, cats and hamsters, are mammals, too.

Some mammals are enormous, and others are tiny. But they all have several things in common:

- They make milk to feed their young.
- They have a backbone.
- They are *warm-blooded*.
- They have fur or hair.

Mammals make milk

Mammals are the only animals that are able to make milk. Mammals feed their babies milk until they are old enough to eat food. Some mammals make milk for their babies for a few weeks, while others make milk for a lot longer.

DID YOU KNOW?

Most of the milk we drink is made by cows to feed their young.

Mice feed their babies milk for a few weeks. Baby elephants live on milk until they are two years old. Once they are two, they start to eat other things but keep drinking milk for another two years.

Mammals have backbones

Mammals have bones inside their bodies. These bones make the mammal's *skeleton*. A skeleton protects parts of the body and helps the animal to move.

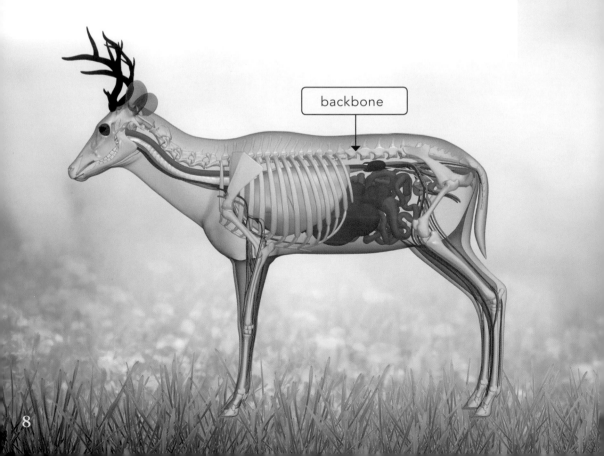

backbone

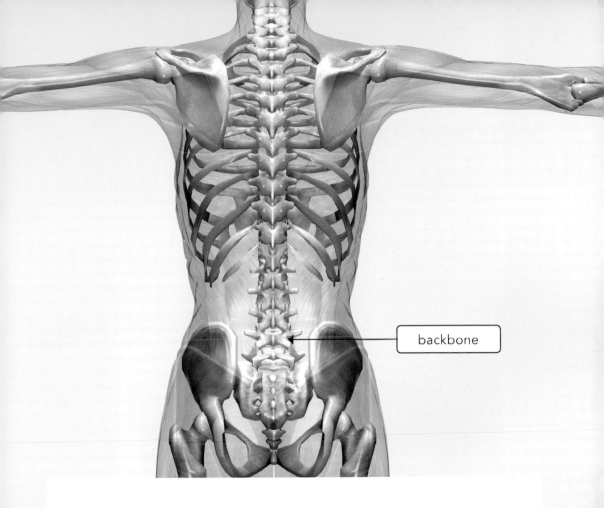

backbone

Every mammal has a group of bones running down the middle of its back. These bones are called the backbone. The backbone is made up of lots of small bones. The backbone allows mammals to bend.

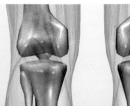

Mammals are warm-blooded

Mammals are warm-blooded. This means that their body *temperature* does not change when the temperature around them changes. A mammal's temperature doesn't get higher on hot days, and it doesn't get lower on cold days.

Mammals have fur or hair

Every mammal has fur or hair. A mammal's fur or hair can be important for different reasons.

Fur can help to keep the animal warm and dry. *Polar bears* have very thick fur that helps to keep them warm. Some *seals* have thick fur, too. Thick fur helps these mammals to survive in very cold places. It also helps to keep them dry.

   Fur can also help an animal to hide. An Arctic fox has fur that is white in winter. The colour of this fox's fur makes it difficult to see in the snow. In the summer, the Arctic fox's fur changes colour. It becomes brown or grey. This makes it easier for the fox to sneak up on other animals when it is hunting for food.

Some mammals have hair that is important for another reason. *Porcupines* are covered with *quills*, which are sharp spikes made of thick hair. The quills grow on the porcupine's back and its tail. The quills protect the porcupine if it is attacked.

You may wonder why whales and dolphins are mammals as they don't seem to have any hair or fur. Some whales and dolphins have hair that falls out soon after they are born. Other whales have a few thick hairs on their heads.

hairs on a whale's chin

Where do mammals live?

Mammals can be found all over the world. Some live on the land, while others live in the water. Mammals live in jungles, *grasslands* and deserts. They live on farms, mountains and in cities. They live in rivers, lakes and oceans, too.

Flying mammals

Some mammals are able to glide or fly through the air. *Sugar gliders* can soar for up to 50 metres (164 feet) to get from one tree to another. A piece of skin joins their front legs to their back legs. When they leap from a branch, this skin is stretched out to form wings. They do not flap, but instead they glide through the air.

  Bats are the only mammals that can really fly. They have very long arm and hand bones. Skin is stretched over these bones to make the bats' wings. Bats are able to flap their wings. They can fly a lot further than sugar gliders can glide.

How are mammals born?

Most mammals give birth to live young. This means that the baby mammal grows inside its mother's body until it is ready to be born. Some baby mammals, such as horses, are quite big when they are born. Baby horses can even get up and walk around soon after being born!

Other mammals, such as *opossums*, are tiny when they are born. Their mother has a special *pouch*. The baby opossums stay inside their pouch for several weeks. They are kept safe and warm inside the pouch.

There is also a small group of mammals that come out of eggs! There are only two animals in this group. They are the platypus and the echidna.

Baby opossums drink milk in their mother's pouch.

All kinds of mammals

There are mammals of all shapes and sizes. One of the smallest mammals is a bat that is so tiny it could sit on your finger. The blue whale is the largest mammal, and it can grow to be as big as three buses!

Mammals are everywhere – underwater, on land and underground! They live in very hot places and in places that are freezing cold. Mammals are a very interesting group of animals!

Glossary

amphibian cold-blooded animal with a backbone; amphibians live in water when young and can live on land as adults

grassland large, open area where grass and low plants grow

opossum animal that lives mostly in trees and carries its young in a pouch

polar bear kind of bear that lives near the North Pole, the northern area of Earth

porcupine small animal covered with sharp hairs called quills

pouch flap of skin that looks like a pocket in which some animals carry their young

quills sharp and stiff needle-like hairs on an animal

seal sea mammal that has thick fur and lives in water

skeleton bones that support and protect the body of a human or other animal

sugar glider small animal found in Australia that is able to glide between trees

temperature how hot or cold something is

warm-blooded having a body temperature that stays about the same all the time

Index